We Were Not Made to Be Small

a collection of dramatics

Taylor Edwards

SYNERGY
PUBLISHING GROUP

BELMONT, NORTH CAROLINA

Dedicated to Aubry, Gracey, and Mallory.
Everything good within me is due to the three of you.
Love, Taylor.

Contents

Section I:

Experior

An ode to Clarity

Lavender & lemon—
a still in the air makes you eager to listen.

Sunbeams, angels incandescent,
illuminate each glitter-dust floating midair.

And the bronze season, your backdrop,
nuzzles your Metis-mind as it spends time tracing creed.

Clarity peeks, with
Her silken strands draping the corner behind you—

Her gaze a visage like lioness nestling leopard cub,
She speaks symphonies aloud:

"Oh, my dear little one, what are you so eager to know?"

The rhythm She coos comforts and cradles
the melange of your mind.

Her essence pushes prisms into the space
(your heart, the room)
bending light in a modus:

INFINITE

"Everything," you respond.

Sunrays splay through the room filling corners
you didn't realize were dark as
Clarity's lips touch to Her cheeks and She dances toward the door.
Turning back, She sings unto you, eyes twinkling,
"Little one, you asked me that last time."

For a moment, uncertainty fills you.
How mighty is the ache for the boundless unknown?

*"Universe does not have the ego for secrets,
small love, just listen."*

Then the Specter, whom you've never
in this life seen prior, is gone.

After some pause, the christened-you opens this page,
humming a song your earthen ears never once heard before.

And, as a since forgotten comfort, we pen the words to its tune.

I grew up around women

I grew up around women,
strong, strong women.

Strong, strong women whose
fervor
durability
wit
were built, together,
at a kitchen table.

The kitchen table,
an island which connects
each mainland we reign.
There the differences in our
becomings
so apparent,
so inconsequential.

Each joan occupies
a seat at the table,
arcing her way through
a life—
voussoirs vanguarding
her way.

I grew up around women,
and when I say
grew,

what I mean is I
sprouted
ached
became
reinvented
reimagined
and became again and again,
around women.

I grew up around women.
I am growing around
these
women.

And, God, I'm so, so thankful.

Goddesses, sisters

I've a Venus.
Her golden hair
hangs
as she beams, unconditional,
meeting all where they stand
and wraps
the world around her finger,
crooning ballads to the wind
on top of seafoam, she sees
the parts of her people
in a way that can only be described as
love inherent.

I've a Hera.
Sharp mind
calculating and reigning
over kingdom,
she safeguards and listens,
always ensuring her
wide eyes are
open and watching,
weighing out all that is
fair and right
and fiercely crests her throne,
mothering us all.

I've a Minerva.
Justice and capability
fuse into each thought
that springs forth

out of her own mind,
safeguarding
with a wisdom,
seeping into every soul,
leaning on her loom,
and weaving a world
that she imagines
and invites us into.

Sometimes we four
stroll down our Appian Way,
and discuss the ways in which
we've spun fate lately.

Inborn freedom

My dearest Adeline,

One of my biggest wishes for you:
never separate from what you innately know.

I see you before my very eyes,
a flipbook of emotions and desires;
you morph and shift in every moment
Unrestrained.

At 15-months, every experience humankind felt
is written on your face—
flashing your ears, pulling your lips, crinkling, flaring,
running your nose
Unabashedly.

When I look at myself in the mirror at 29-years,
I see decades of hiding from that which is inside me—
numbing, an absence of reaction,
a poker face, one stoic presence
Unobtrusive.

One glance at you and I ache to unteach myself
a lifetime of shrinkage.
In your body, you are free.

With a hope that traverses between us,
I bid you never are forced to
Unlearn,

for you will have never strayed
from your inborn freedom.

Love forever,
Your T.T.

Experior, act I

Up until the very recent past,
I did an excellent job of
living,
and working,
and being
. . . without trying.

On the road map of Life,
I had a one-way lane,
insipid straight path,
Destination: Where You're Going,
Starting Point: Where You're At.

Detours be damned.
There was no work-in for
trustless-yen.
I would best the ETA;
I reveled in being
one
minute
under.

Experior, act II

The Fear of wanting more
strikes sharp,
quick, short.

Fleeting, if you let it.

What's the alternative, though?
Finding a face in the mirror,
staring back,
unrecognized?
Following you along every
insouciant milestone,
Fool's paradise?

Wafting out candle's
end of life,
counting years in
would-have-dones and
almost-dids?

Taking into account, Fear's a lot
less painful than
self-unawareness,
joyless-goals,
alright-birthdays,
always-missing-the-mark,
even at the end.

With these scenes in my head,
the ETA climbed

as I sat, rigid.

The next Where I'm Going
was growing impatient:
"We have a reservation,"
it said.

The road map I fawn-followed
led to toasting flutes with
business suits in
a garish restaurant:
revolting.

Volte-face I turned,
met my own eyes
and thought,

"She looks like a more fun time."

Experior, act III

Unrolling the map,
I took a bigger look at the picture.
Alpha and omega, the journey was
perfectly derivative
and completely uninspired.

In an inaugural rebellion,
I flipped the map
on its back, searching,
and found firebranded
CREATOR: NOT ME.

Trying is toiling—
without a safety net.

Trying doesn't have an assurance.

There is no variable which
ousts failure from the table.

Do I dare be uncharted?

One final glance at the
insidious emblem,
I decided I did.

I packed up the map
and its guarantees:
promotions, raises, rings, sheenier things—
I set them ablaze,

and scrawled out a new one:
You will experience everything.

And I did.

Now the scroll I follow
is written in my own hand,
compass internal.
We have a great time in our
often rerouting,
always ending up
where we want to be,
day-to-day joy of the
decision to move.

Prodeamus et experior . . .

Conversations with myself: part I

Earlier today someone asked me if I was "okay,"
and thoughts cascaded against gray matter,
as expectant eyes awaited an admittance
my
soul
did
not
validate.

Discount my own account,
my amygdala is no longer trusted
when the eyes of another,
assessing, burrows in my lobe.

"Yeah, I think so?"

The someone who asked me
looked
me
up
and
down
with a hint of their own
righteous justification
and then, finally, responded,
"okay."

Perceived perception, twisted and turned, like a weapon:
No one asks you if you're okay,
if they think you're okay.

Now here, I am speculating,
appraising,
all my indicators
of authenticating
my own trust.

If I haven't portrayed okay, then am I okay?
Help me.

At an invocation,
my bones lighten.

Black ink on white page
offers a prism,
filtering my shades of self
in clarity called forth:

"Observing a one-off
assessment of you,
revering it as fact, and
then spear-heading
the onus
and crafting a
plan
of
attack:
What a night you've had,
my love.

I see you spinning
like Giselle's pirouette,

but you're in
the
wrong
scene.

'Am I okay?' isn't the
question,
burden,
plea—
no, love,
what you're spinning
around is the mourning of
verdict: *misunderstood.*

What if I told you you feel
misunderstood
because you are
misunderstood.
And, there's
nothing
abominable
about that.

The secret of it all?
Nuanced is misunderstanding; it is both
inconsequential
and
everlasting.

Every breathing being walks
into tiny, walled rooms with
the vastness of the Universe

beating inside of them,
cradle to grave.

The knowing of everything
and nothing,
crashing against one another
within
and
in between
each person
and people.

Understanding is miracle
on the divine, golden chance it happens.

I beg of you:
do not move
like a leaf in the
wind of the
world for
every
single
ping.

The Universe inside of you
is so much greater than that.

You are loved, accepted, appreciated,
and, also, less importantly,
okay.

Stop being so hard on yourself."

Conversations with myself: part II

Fear penetrates my skin.
An unknown opponent
lies in wait.
Its face, shrouded;
its name, shadowed.

I'm not sure the foe, the problem, the upset
that wishes to upturn, throw off
my aim.

Their raison d'etre met
in the expanse of my mind—
horribilities imagined within those confines,
strike throughgoing
simply in their expanse.

Help me.

With a desperate plea
penned on page,
the body shifts.

In curl and loop an answer evoked comes forth:

"What would your day be like today
if you allowed yourself, reminded yourself,
every moment is not beholden to
exploration of deep, psychological self-inspection,
or deliberate self-rejection?

Refuse, instead, the concept of
maintaining a Kármán-line view,
all the time.

Darling, in fact, you mustn't.

Three hundred thousand feet
above the ground
can only be visited
when your vibration is equal
to that of which you go.
In a disposition of disarray,
all you can do is freeze.

Stoic and statuesque,
in an altitude not meant for your state,
of course you will conjure
wretched phantasms.

Instead, today, just today,
take today's view, please, my love.
There is only today, today.

Pellucid are your nerves,
unbalanced on a ledge.
It's okay to want everything,
want the cosmos,
and be so afraid to make the move for it.

I see you.

I see your continual push, your *don't-stop-keep-moving-strive-for-better-automatic-reroute-when-the-world-leaves-you-disappointed-resilience-as-the-only-option-so-let's-jump-straight-there-because-we-don't-have-time-to-pause-beautiful-giving-thoughtful-soul-of-just-a-human-being-that-you-are.*

I see you.
And, in today there are no nemeses,
no ignoble foes to account for,
hair-on-edge.
Nothing guards, through promise of death,
the treasure of what you intend."

Ink runs dry,
Peace swells forth.
A final writ:

"Be still, then march. Over, and over again."

We were not made to be small

When I'm the best of who I am,
my soul has no size tag,
appraising:
> *Small*
> *Medium*
> *Large.*

My soul itself
is endless, immeasurable.
My soul takes up space and shifts its being
from every cardinal direction:
> *VAST*

[The other day, I met a lady in the bathroom. I slunk from the stall and willed her space she already took up, in front of the ceramic sink. As she dried her weighty hands against scratchy cardboard paper towels, we exchanged]

ME, SUCKING IN AND SQUEEZING PAST HER, PARCELING OUT
THE HALF BREATH I HELD:
Excuse me.

LARGE WOMAN IN THE BATHROOM:
This bathroom is small. Because that's what they say women
should be.

ME, SHRINKING CLOSER AGAINST BONE:
I know.

LARGE WOMAN IN THE BATHROOM:
I guess they don't know us.

ME, ALLOWING THE DOOR TO SLAM AGAINST HER FACE:
[sheepishly]
I know . . .

FUCK THE PATRIARCHY
IS ETCHED IN EVERY FABRIC OF MY LIFE.
WHY, THEN, AM I AFFRONTED
WHEN A WOMAN LOOKS TO ME AS HER REFLECTION,
ADMONISHING THE POWER THAT DICTATES
WHAT BODIES SHOULD BE?
THE BODIES THAT WE DON'T HAVE?

"Women should be small"
is the biggest lie
I've let rot in my stomach . . .
The one thing I've yet to
purge
out of me.

Thank you, large woman in the bathroom, for your vastness.
I'm still sometimes forgetting:
We Were Not Made to Be Small.

(I'm sorry I slammed the door in your face.)

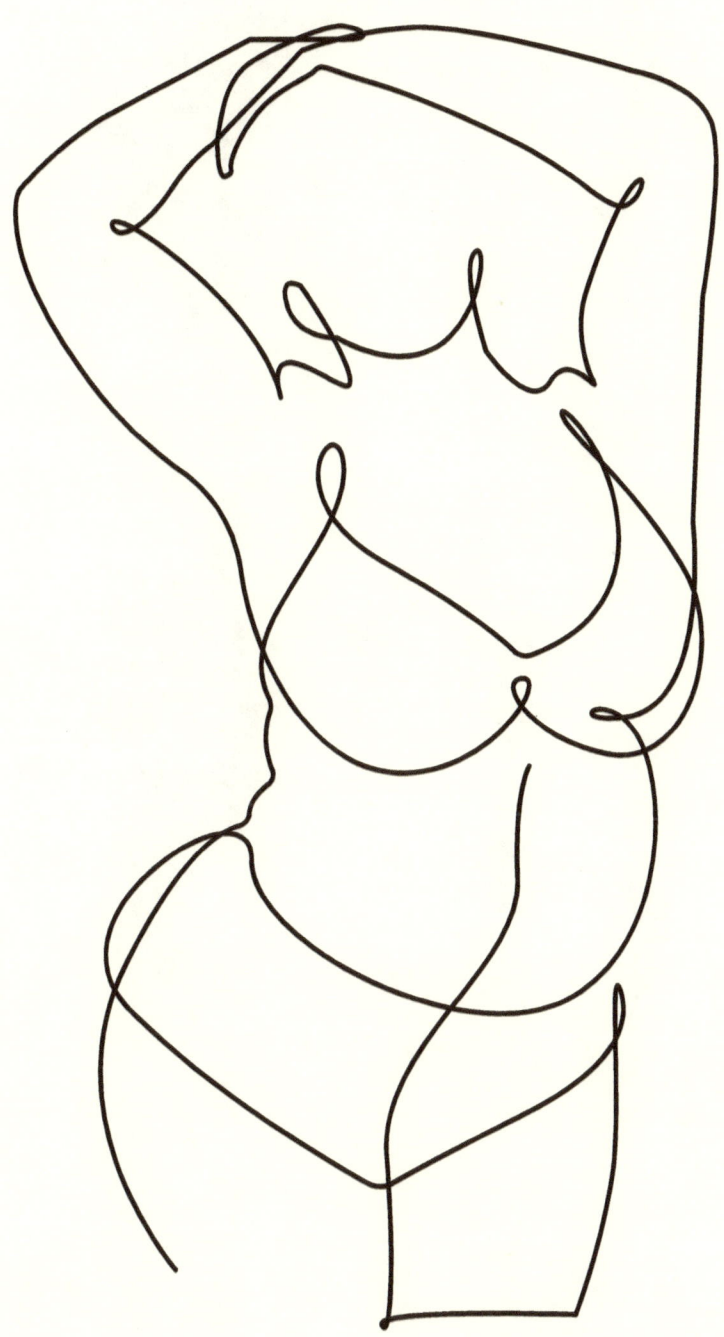

Section II:

A face like a
wet weekend

Crashing

I'm vexed
with myself.
My inability to
fucking relax
in its real, true, genuine way.

(bones-at-rest-jaw-slack-muscles-loose-fists-sans-flexion)

Because crashing isn't relaxing.
I've just claimed "relax"
to mask "crash."
When what I really mean is:

(to-hide)

Unaffected

There's a box I wear around me.
Glass,
smooth surface,
completely impenetrable
division
between me
and the outside world.

Outside voices can be heard.
They are easily turned off,
simple as the flip of a switch.

Chatter about politics beside me,
spoken by gruff old men,
without an ounce of empathy,
who have the volume turned down.

And I'm cut off from a reaction
to that of which they speak.

I can see through the box,
a prison partition,
my eyes aren't prevented
from observing.

I notice a plant at the window,
dry and wilted,
doubtful it's been watered in weeks.
But it can fade with the box as my aid—
I don't have to see it.

There are a couple reasons
for the box.
Chiefly, there are a couple *feelings*,
the box provides . . .
useful to me at certain times:
Peaceful.
Steady.
Unaffected.

---

unaffected *adjective*
/ˌʌnəˈfektɪd/
/ˌʌnəˈfektɪd/
**unaffected (by something) not changed or influenced
by something; not affected by something**

Yet, I wonder, on a day
when the box feels . . .
a little more numbing than useful:
could unaffectedness be doing me harm?

Granted: it feels safer,
more resolved,
quieter,
than when I'm unveiled,
skin sitting in air
shared by others.

But, what if *unaffected* meant middle of the road?

Neither exuberant
nor devastated,
unaffected correlated to

independence
and solitude,
as if I knew more than the world itself,
the world's problems
could not coerce me into emotion.

Unaffected is the absence of affect.
And is the absence of affect,
just not to care?

Unaffected:
I employ it often
in the face of uncertainty.

Affected, though?
Well, that makes me
hold my breath.

When affected, concentration can falter,
breeding imperfection and
mistake, plates would drop,
the tightrope would fall—
engaging is draining,
and fuck, wouldn't the
other shoe
just

        D
           R
              O
                  P

I mean.
That doesn't happen in the box, right?

The idea of affectedness
festers in my stomach like acid—
a literal inability to
digest this foreign concept.

But what if acid could
transform into butterflies?

Could my whole soul *affectedly* light up?

> **affected** *transitive verb*
> /əˈfektɪd/
> **to produce an effect upon (someone or something)**

Facade

"I don't give a fuck."
A mask I wore.
But deep inside,
care simmered
in wait to rise again.

A face like a wet weekend

I don't know where to turn
or where to go.

Being around someone feels exhausting.
Not being near someone feels terrifying.

This dilemma haunts me
on weekends.

Aching, no matter the scenery,
depression curses me stagnant
and anxiety begs me to frenzy.

A face like a wet weekend,
I cry for the push/pull,
back/forth,
up/down,
within the prison of my mind.

Because being around someone feels exhausting,
and not being near someone feels terrifying.

Come back to bed

Come back to bed.
She says
with a voice like
guilt,
simple syrup,
and
sinking lead.

Sleep here with me.
She bargains,
as the load I'm carrying
doubles, triples, amplifies
in size.

Just let me comfort you.
She seeps,
presence looming and oozing
on and through and around
stained sheets.

What would you do without me?
She chides,
as I succumb,
overtaken,
turning on a heel and
crumbling
atop cotton confinement.

Rolling over, I make myself small against
her, the darkness of the room

helping me forget there was ever
a light to my eyes.

An ember of quickening,
despised for its own potential,
I vow to Tomorrow:
I'll do better.

You can't leave me!
A banshee,
she squalls.

Depression's a
jealous bitch.

Piggy bank promise

Tiny hands dialing,
no credit card, but
all my coins
pledged to save
starving hearts
across a distant screen.

I *rocked* and *bawled*,
wrapped in arms,
too small to hold
a world of pain.
At five years old,
I asked:

How can we not help?

Love-child of indecision

Most of my days are spent on the precipice of "low."
One wrong move, one misstep,
and the world darkens.

Shoulders up, jaw clenched, breath held,
grasping for every card contained in my back pocket.
Maybe I can find new cards,
I think.

The stack grows thinner and thinner.

Some of my days are spent on the exhalation of "high":
No wrong moves; all good steps,
my world is bright lights and warm Sun on expectant skin,
laughter supernova across my face,
love and kindness and compassion and home.
When I am good, I am oh-so-good.

If grace is the marriage between the "low" and the "high,"
am I the love-child of indecision?
Or the bastard-child of unacceptance?

In my world, opposites don't attract.
They split.
They diverge.
Binaries polarize.

I am learning how love-children and bastards live in-between. I've no home yet.

Section III:

Discourse

Perpetual way

You're a fresh breath of air
right before a strong rain.
A glass half full
in the perpetual way.

Your million personalities,
and those discerning eyes,
you came into my world,
you came as a surprise.

Hundreds of hours
wrapped up in
conversations with you,
the way you talk is
something brand new.

Tangled up like pretzels
and listening to music
on the couch,
slowly but surely—
you're erasing my doubts.

My anxiety sometimes
rages, in leaps and bounds, but
feeling you,
in a moment—
it puts me on
stable ground.

The way you tend to your home,

dance so light on your feet,
set aside a plant
(you said it was just for me),
brings a lightness
into my heart
I can't help but want to keep.

Seeing you at the counter,
feeding your crew,
or hearing you strum
on your guitar anew,
you're safety and warmth,
and softness and strength,
I'm so looking forward
to see what you reap.

From your plans
you've enacted
to your dreams
that you've planted,
you're building our world,
a world that's enchanted.

Twelve grapes under the table

Before we pulled suitcases
down cobblestone
and shouted auld lang syne
down Charlotte's streets,
we sat under the table,
in a sacred holiness
shrouded by tablecloth,
with a bottle of Clicquot and
twelve grapes.

Stuffed them in our mouths,
let them fester in bellies already full,
and confessed to each other
wishes
we hoped the new year
would bring.

What I didn't tell either of you—
each grape I bit down the middle,
split skin and savored,
with teeth against taste,
I wished the same wish:
Being here.
Over and over again.

A soft place to land

My body is a home,
a soft place to land for those lucky enough
to live there.

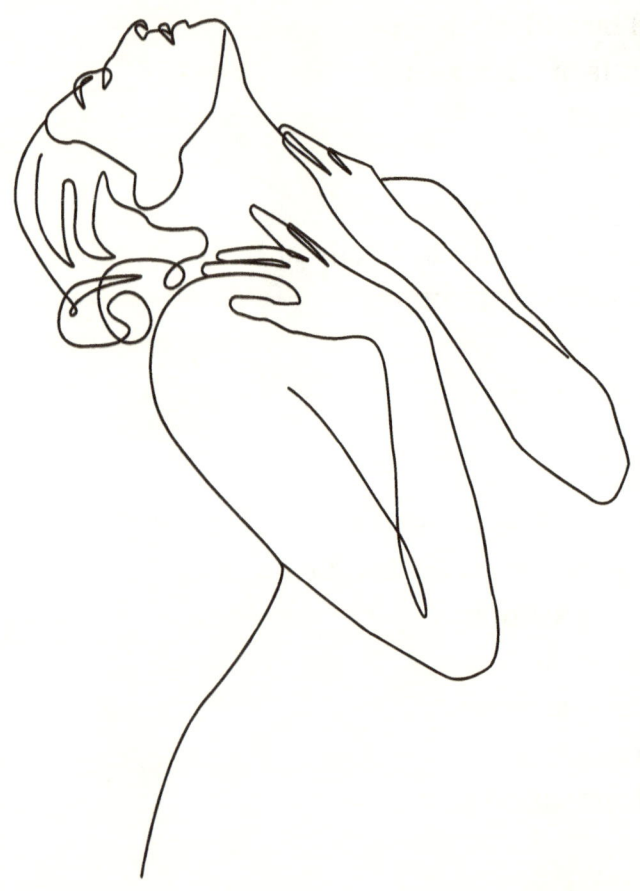

Not an arrow, but an erosion

Love doesn't strike like an arrow.
Cupid is a cherub,
looking to lovers
like children looking to mothers:
simply.

Limited and lacking,
this above strike
misses
its
mark.

Love doesn't strike
like an arrow
because there's no sequence,
Point A to Point B,
for it to follow.

Straight lines
are never
directives
in love.

Instead, love erodes;
it compresses.
Every single day
more is unearthed.

If we wiggled and rubbed,
massaged

along the ground,
we'd go as far as the earth's core, eventually.
A white hot center
enlivening us all.

Care to caress the ground with me?
We'll fall in love this way.

A letter, part I

If I wrote a letter to the girl I *feel things for*
I would start out by saying . . .
I'm not in love.

Don't freak out about the absurdity
of a hand-written note,
the dated wax seal pressed
upon the envelope,
or the scent of patchouli
that drips off the page.

I'd like to think by now you know,
nine times out of ten,
my dramatics are
just for show.

If I wrote a letter to this girl,
I think it would be full of
confetti moments,
floating together to make
a celebration.

Shared mornings and nights,
evenings and afternoons
dusted with one-liners
and photographs.

If I wrote a letter to my girl,
I'd try to maintain confidence throughout.

Because I know there's a billion and one
shredded bits of reasons
why this shouldn't happen,
can't be,
won't work.

But, if she wanted it to?
I'd figure that part out.

If I wrote a letter to you,
I'd scatter in our commonalities
and the way you make me laugh.
Throw in bits of your sass,
and I'd tell you I reveled in
your expression
when I gave it back.
Confessing to you all the while,
how every day I remind myself that
I have to slow down.

I'm writing a letter to the girl *I feel things for,*
and, I'm not in love.
But, I could be.

A letter, part II

In a second letter, I'd write about
watching *some Disney movie* with our friends,
jigsawed on the couch.
My jigsaw piece hugged toward hers
as we held hands under the blanket.
I squeezed her hand
every time I laughed,
and she squeezed back.

I left as the hero returned
the costume
to her father's closet.
I pulled onto the road thinking,
"I'm going to fall in love with her one day."

It's the contradiction of what I thought
my entire life.
Up until now,
falling off the tightrope
wasn't an option,
because spinning plates
atop sticks
gripped in my hand
was reality.

And, dammit, if I wouldn't make it
to the end of that rope.

What if the
other side,

with its steps,
and downward progression
towards safety
wasn't the goal after all?

                              Could maybe I float through?

Desire

Open wide: g(r)asp what's whirled,
if it's a fight you're looking for, that isn't what's in store.

You're but the Earth,
and I the Sky.
An ever consuming ingestion,
two deities charged in desire.

My favorite part of us, though?
The lightning strike that zaps when we collide.

It cuts through, hotter than Sun—
if that was the God they were looking to worship,
they picked the wrong one.

Will you prick my skin?
Can I feel your spark?

My favorite version of myself
lives in the glass
that fused
the night I hit your sand.

Discourse

You invited me into a new language,
one I'd never heard before,
and now mastered, since.

Syllables roll around my mouth
exploding in stars and color,
no space for connotation,
our lexicon is my safe haven.

An isolate parlance,
our lingomorphistic love
lives in the palette.

Flat full tongue,
caresses the back of your teeth,
I moved in as we spoke oaths.

Cross your heart,
hope to die,
if ever I
linguicide.

Section IV:

Queens Mountain

Queens Mountain

In the words I write now,
I invoke Terentia, Queen of the Mountain,
speaker of love,
beauty unparalleled,
allow me to share your story,
your story of sacrifice for your home, your kinsmen.
Oh, great muse, fill my hands with your
words and share the song through this portal,
so that all can know your truth and memory,
washing away the dust that befall your being
and bring forth into this day
the sureness of your spirit that
lives within your mountain now,
that never left those stones,
only just forgotten for
far too long.

May it be forgotten no more.

CANTOS I:
In my city, there's a watchtower of a woman.
She fills the sky with the rise of her breasts,
the spill of her belly,
the flat of her thighs.
Sometimes, even the forest dances
to the rhythm of her breath.

Her consistency has almost made her unrecognizable.
You can't see the forest for the trees—
a locution that doesn't touch

her absolution.
No, here, you can't see the woman for the mountain.

Geologists dated her as older than millennia.
Storytellers aged her as more ancient than that.

Before she was the Earth, she was flesh.

It was her feet that once paved the way
for rivets and rivers to burrow in this town, Vasiliakon.
Before she was stone, she was Terentia.

CANTOS II:
Daughter of a healer, Terentia loved her people.
She moved through her village like a feather in air.
She registered the footsteps of each
villager before seeing their face,
knowing everyone by pace alone.

Often spotted sitting by the Vasiliakonen well,
her long, dark hair
washed along stone as she sat
criss-crossed, hearing people of the town
share their stories of each day.

Each child and adult loved Terentia
as their village heart-healer.
Much like her father,
Terentia made things better.
Her father specialized in
remedies and herbs for that which
the eye could see, broken.

Terentia, instead, fixed things that couldn't be touched:
a swirling mind plagued with loss,
a heavy heart infected by love unrequited,
a timid gut bruised with confidence taken,
she had the panacea for all.
Terentia whispered words as spells,
easing all who came to her well.

The children, especially, sought Terentia's comfort.
One morning, grass still fresh with dew,
Terentia found Foviehre—
smallest son of the butcher Thrishme.
He was Terentia's favorite of all the village children,
although she would never show it.
With a sensitive soul that reminded her of her own,
Terentia consoled Foviehre
on days of great sensitivity.
He would become her one day:
a figure of comfort within the town.
For only a soul that felt so much,
so big,
could ever stand witness to others.

One day, Foviehre was
crying at the well,
lonely in his bones.
Tears fell down his small face,
streaking innocence in misunderstanding
as he held a daisy blossom.
The blossom's yellow clenched so tight
it almost dyed his fingers.
Terentia murmured words of

love, acceptance, belonging.
Encouragements of a love
so loud that Foviehre
forgot his fears and
joined the other children, smiling,
as they played toy soldiers together until dusk.

CANTOS III:
Terentia brought kinsmanship, love,
and a listening ear for all who drew near;
she was the gem of the village.
All followed her.

Peace is easy to miss when it's all that's known,
and during that well-wishing era, amity reigned in totality.

Yet, one day at the well, Terentia held
the fear poured into her by friends.
Their mouths twisted and contorted to repeat
a name that was foreign, blunt to hold on the tongue:
Oarcx.

Antithesis to Vasiliakon, the Oarcx were
an army of evil-men,
burning and sieging each town they encountered.
Villagers told Terentia horrors of legend,
that which the crows carried.
As village-friends sat at the well,
each took turns confessing the truest terror:
The Oarcx were tasked with conquering Vasiliakon next.

She sat and rocked her people

as they congregated around the well—
rapt to her words of comfort.
The stone's hardness pressed against
each thigh, juxtaposing the clearness of air
and siren song of words as she
held their fears and exchanged them
for tokens of hope, comfort, peace, goodness,
so that each person left feeling lighter
for a moment, and even a few after.

As the last body made their way home
against soft grass blades that tickled toes,
Terentia was left to ruminate in solitude:
What would come of Vasiliakon?

Her hand dropped down the well,
churning and swirling water
as she wondered.

She spoke promises of hope and safety
to her people earlier,
but all the while she held silent internal thoughts:
what if there was no safety to be found?
In their soft homebeds, it was rare a home that held
sword, bow, armor, shield—
her father was in the minority with his hunter's bow.
If foe were to enter, how could they survive?

Heavier with stacked worries,
Terentia made her way home, a push of
tears behind her face and the
twist of turmoil behind her trunk.

CANTOS IV:
As the days passed, the name Oarcx practiced
against native tongue and the wind
carried word of villages near
overtaken, razed, torn
by the evil-men, motivated by greed and
the alien concept of more,
thieves of joy, and murderers of content.

Each morning-sun rose with Terentia
as she moved through town
to arrive at the well.
She soon replaced her steadfast hope with
internal questions,
wondering the extent of truth she heard,
and how each tree, home, neighbor might be changed
if that which lurked stopped lurking and arrived.

CANTOS V:
A fortnight later, Terentia was tending titan arum
when her ears picked up
the distinctive putter
of Gaaria Greatmother,
a village elder blessed with visions,
steering behind her.

As Gaaria made her way down the path,
her figure half-hobbled over an oak tree cane.
Her snow-hair rippled down in a braid atop
furrowed brow that preened over
clouded eyes.
Terentia could feel the weight of what

the Seerer carried.

Wiping her hands and holding her breath,
Terentia met Gaaria and saw
despair weighing within the woman,
so strong Terentia nearly dropped
right then and there.

The heaviness of Gaaria's spirit trammeled the air.
She reached for Terentia's hands and clasped them,
holding on with a grip that was barely a grasp:
"Terentia, my strength, there is a burden within me.
If there was any other way, I would not rest it upon you.
What I disclose to you now, please know . . .
I would keep it buried if I could."

"The Oarcx, I have seen, will be here in but one sunrise.
And with their visit, they will ignite our homes,
demolish our structures, massacre our elders,
and enslave the rest of our people."

Lifting a hand to silence Terentia's coming protest,
the old woman
carried on, body shaking and breath struggled:
"It is true. The vision.
I tossed and fought all night against
images of atrocities clawing within my mind—
everything that is to be done to the town
appeared before my eyes.
There is neither Hell nor hound
I fear more than what I witnessed.
As Sun rose this morning, I was still wrestling with the

premonition, fearing it would be the last sunrise.
There was only one thing that stopped the
story within my mind's eye, only one thing
able to stop the Oarcx from fully overtaking Vasiliakon."

Tears pricked Terentia's eyes and
her body flushed.

"It is you," Gaaria said.

"No," Terentia's frail voice eked out.
"Impossible—"

With this announcement, the Seerer attempted a breath,
ragged in her bones.
As a testimony to the fierceness still fighting
in the Greatmother's body, Gaaria continued on.

"Your face appeared in my vision and all else stopped.
The horror, atrocity, the evil-men themselves
were swallowed into the ground as soon as
you appeared.
The Gods above have shared to me that you are the
only way to halt the attack."

Beats passed between the two women.
Terentia believed Gaaria's visions—
they'd never proved false before.
She trusted Gaaria even more than
her own desire, fervent and raging,
not to trust.

Gaaria stood silently and
witnessed the prophecy
(that she so hated to deliver!)
streaking across Terentia's ashen face.

Finally, with despair
thick in her throat, Terentia asked
the questions that
echo through the heart
of every mortal
in every moment
before they choose
to accept or decline
their destiny:
"How? How is there any shred of possibility I can?"

With her message delivered and Gaaria spent,
the Greatmother heaved one full and desperate breath,
eyes seeing nothing but the entirety of Terentia's soul,
and attempted to answer the unfathomable:
"I don't know, but you will."

And with those final words
hanging upon air,
laden wretched with heaviness
that an answer
solely hinging on pointed responsibility
and doubt brings,
the Seer was gone—
Terentia entranced, alone,
attempted to swallow the gravis brought.

CANTOS IV:
A duty doled, Terentia allowed the morning Sun
to propel her muscles and routine to
pull her along
her daily route to the well.
During her walk, Terentia
witnessed her neighbors mimicking-normal
down roadways:

Saarahan gripping wicker basket,
delivering eggs to market,
eyes searching each face,
double-checking recognition.

A hooded Esthierre
clutching chrysanthemums in fist,
leaving petals in her trail,
no awareness of what she was leaving behind.

Umbreh locked in hands with her new-husband,
yet their bodies were ill-attuned to
collective direction,
almost diverging at the fork ahead.

Each neighbor greeted Terentia,
words in passing,
with breath held
involuntarily.
They no longer dared to
invoke evil by speaking their fears aloud,
for the Seer's words had gotten around.

Each neighbor held silence,
waiting to hear an alien
war-cry trumpet ring—
the sound never yet
echoed against their valleys and hills.

Upon Terentia finally meeting her well,
she fell onto its bench,
drained.

Unlike days prior, no one sought
Terentia that afternoon:
fear was heavy over the village, and
despite its need, community was too tiring
in the face of what could be ahead.

CANTOS VI:
Her night was spent, fitful.
Tossing and turning skin against blanket,
Terentia fought back tears of desperation
as her restless mind imagined visions of
war.

Sleep wouldn't save her, and in that moment,
Terentia believed nothing could.
Hours fell along like grains of sand
piling time, hoarding it,
precious moments left before
Gaaria's prophecy was to begin.

When Moon met Sun
and the Earth began to awaken,

Terentia, still in the Hell of her conscious,
finally cried out:
"Am I to go into battle?
Slay the army?
Create a diversion—
the only chance for us to succeed?
What do I do?
If this be my burden, my one true charge,
how do I know?
Please Gods, lead me!"

And, with that cry, the virgin war-trumpet
rang for its first time.

CANTOS VII:
The trumpet, a Godsend if it wasn't
such a harbinger,
put Terentia back in her body, momentarily,
and pulled her from the misery her mind inhabited.

Father.

Ears picking up on the stomp-stomp-stomp of invaders,
Terentia emerged out of bed with the only
impetus that could cut her fear:
her father.

Feet flying through fields, she dare not
breathe until she saw the
familiar face
already waiting by an open door.

Lunging into arms almost too feeble to hold,
she gripped her father with all her might.
"Father, the Oarcx are here.
We must go to the villagers.
I don't know what from there, but we dare not
meet this alone."

A nod alongside a reach for his
hunter's bow and arrow
was all the response Terentia received from him.
As the gray of the morning saw
signs of light emerge,
they took to the town.

With her father's hand in hers,
Terentia and he walked roads their soles knew
through many seasons.
Those familiar drops, still standing at ducts
from the night prior, threatened to stream
down Terentia's face as she confessed:
"Father, we're walking toward our death."

To that, her father finally spoke:
"Aren't we always, Terentia,
daughter that I have been gifted to love for
nineteen sun-trips now?
Aren't we always walking toward our deaths?"

Continuing, he spoke, louder now,
"I've been placed on this land with a great luck.
A great ability to help others,
a great fortune to be helped.

If today is the day that this soul-cycle ends,
I am saddened, yes,
for I would've liked to stay here longer.

But when your mother died, Terentia,
I felt like that was death on Earth.
I imagine this will be much like that,
if today is the day our earthen selves cease,
there will be great fear, great pain.
There will be the great
disbelief that there is no hope,
and no Greater Beings there to
care for us.
It will finally be at the break of utter defeat
we see, then,
the Sun rise again.

Know now, my daughter, there are
Greater Beings that care for you,
and they won't leave you today.
Neither will I.
And, somewhere, against a time and space
we cannot comprehend . . .
there will be a heavenly Sun that rises for us again."

Stopping before the villages entryway,
Terentia and her father stilled themselves.
Bracing the tears once more, she refused
to submit to them in her last moments with her father.

"I believe you, father."
Wrapping her arms around him, she

prayed to Gods above,
the Greater Beings he invoked,
and everything she believed in:
Whatever happens, let it be quick.

With that final thought in mind,
Terentia and her father entered the village.

CANTOS VIII:
Unlike anything ever witnessed before,
a melee of villagers crowded the streets.
Most were preparing for battle with tears
and wails.

Makeshift armor, weapons, and shields donned
the villagers as war does when it is unfit
for those who don it.

As Terentia was trying to help
string together swords from garden sticks,
she heard the cries of children from beyond.

Little imps, they climbed to the tallest tree
in Vasiliakon to see the invaders on the horizon.
They themselves arrived as a miniature army
back to the town-center to tell of their arrival.

"They broke the parapet!" one child cried.
"They're coming!"

Terentia, having to see it with her own eyes,
ran toward the broken parapet's direction and

propelled herself up a tree.

They were here.

CANTOS IX:
In great number, the evil-men were
entering the town with weaponry plenty.
No garden tools in sight on their end,
they each had a sword and shield on body.
Howling in tune with their war-step,
they outnumbered the town by multitudes.
Faces painted red and stomping in full force,
Terentia knew these men were demons
hellbent on destroying everything in the world
that could be good,
simply for the sport of it all.

Feeling bark against her leg, Terentia slid down the tree,
running back to her community
with no thought as to only fly there.
Her head empty and moving only by the
propellent of fear, she registered nothing.

That is, until, she saw men and boys of her village
creeping toward that which she just left.
Farmers and growers
were nothing and everything
in comparison to the Oarcx.

Her people were nothing formidable in violence or atrocity,
but everything good that was the antithesis of the Oarcx's evil.
Males of every age were in lead, with women following behind,

touting even less in weaponry.

One small figure stayed on the fringe between men and boys,
if you could even call it a figure,
for anything human had been wrung from its body:
Foviehre, Terentia's favorite,
shook with every step
as he was forced forward.

It was at that moment, the first arrow fell.

CANTOS X:
Flashbacks shielded Terentia's eyes
from reality and
toward the past.

She saw Foviehre over the years,
his sensitivities
becoming more managed,
still feeling, yet now not drowned by them.

Her father, she remembered from when
she was but a child.
He was so tall and so strong:
knowing everything,
and never growing ill when
she wanted to know everything, too.

Gaaria, stepping in and loving her,
teaching her as only a mother could,
when her mother was taken from her,
too young.

Saarahan, Esthierre, Umbreh:
every soul
held space in her mind.
She felt the ties that rooted her
to the village and its people,
the ties that were grounding, stable,
no matter what horrors faced ahead.

She couldn't let the Oarcx demolish
what she held so, so dear.

CANTOS XI:
It was then that the water behind her eyes,
dammed for so long,
broke forth for this damned plight.
How was Terentia to prevent it?
She couldn't let the Oarcx overtake her village.

In an abyss she never knew she could visit,
despair overtook her as a visceral scream
broke through her body's frame and
wailed
toward the open air.

The loudness of her voice halted time for a moment.
Everything and everyone stopped.
The richness of her wail was a
sound that every soul recognized:
a woman despondent,
a woman hopeless,
a woman enraged.

Allowing the power of her voice to
continue, her battle-cry echoed through
the valleys and streams.
Her tears leaving their own ocean
behind her,
in one fluid motion she grabbed
her father's bow from his hands and
ran.

CANTOS XII:
Terentia ran toward the demons
with a speed no other entity could possess,
the bow and arrow in her hands
still alien, but grafting to her
tighter and tighter with each leap.

Raging and racing toward the battle front,
she saw the full horror of what the Oarcx unleashed.
Her sapphire skies and malachite fields,
all were war-washed in blood.

With the brava of an Athenian hero,
she brought herself further into the fold of fray
and pulled the arrow back along its bow.

"Gods, help me," she thought.

In a golden moment, she felt strength possess her in a way
she never felt within her bones before.
Shifting hip to pull the arrow back further,
she sent it with flight toward an Oarcx warrior,

blackened eyes and red-painted face,
gaping at her—
she felt certain that her arrow would pierce.

She never found out if that arrow made its mark.

CANTOS XIII:
In a microsecond within her glory,
a demon-foe pushed its sword into her open side,
extended from her bow's travel,
and pushed metal into her body,
flashing eons of pain as she
fell to the ground.

Tears that never stopped flowing,
fell harder.

The war continued around her body
as she lay dying.

Screams amplified, her senses only heightened in
her oncoming death, she could make out each
footfall of her loved ones.

Each breath billowed pain
in beats she could have never fathomed.

The quickness she prayed for prior was not to come.

Faintly, a memory of her father came to her
clouded mind: the Sun rises again, somewhere.
She allowed a trace of a smile to tug at her face.

I love my Father, his wisdom, his presence.

Body sinking heavier onto soil,
she could almost see the glow of the morning-sun
he talked about.
Thank Gods, dying is almost done.

CANTOS XIV:
The glow brightened from behind her,
and in an attempt to meet the Heavenly he described,
she put forth the effort it took to turn her head to the side,
seeking the divinity that could be her new home.

Eyes searching for the light behind,
mind clouded,
she could not swear it, but—
the well?

Was it the well the Sun was springing forth from?

Her beloved well, amassed in a light—
no, it was *the* light, wasn't it?—
illuminated the village from its bottomless source.
Her limp gaze happened upon Foviehre:
he was beside the well now, index finger extended.
Poor Foviehre, he sees me here, bloodied, dying,
he shouldn't have to see it—
no one should.

Yet, the light grew brighter from the well.
She could even feel it on skin now . . .
what was once numbed from wound.

Her skin was glowing too?
And shaking?
Not seizures of death, no her body was
vibrating, full?

No.
Not her body—
the ground.

The ground itself was shaking.

And she was floating!

Is this my great ascension?
She thought as she felt the
ground pushing her body,
up, up, up higher.

But, yet, was everyone ascending?
As she mustered strength to turn her head around,
every villager she loved was rising, too.

Their faces, mystified, *what are they saying?*
Are they calling my name?

Thoughts hazy, Terentia could only observe
those around her—
their faces widened,
questioning how?

And, wait, she thought—
the entirety of her town was climbing, higher, higher,

above the ground,
but also with it?
And the light, Gods, it feels so warm.

The light was billowing wider and wider,
every pore of her body was filled with it,
as the voices continued around her,
amplified,
by their sadness.

No, not sadness. They were cries of joy.

At that moment, Terentia's mind ceased,
and she was gone.

CANTOS XV:
Well, not gone, really.

What her body once was had now transformed.
Her body, now a mountain holding her people,
safe.

As the ground lifted, her body immersed into
geography and she became a mountain,
housing those she held dear.
Bones bending with breadth,
she bent but she did not break.
Her spine elongated,
her stomach enlarged,
everything within her pushed
more, more, more
in the manner of

a woman who loves.

As her body expanded and became
structure, her final images,
joyous, were of Oarcx falling off her as
the plains and layers
created a range where
they were not welcome at all.

Although Terentia was never seen
in human form
by her beloved neighbors again,
they lived on her every day
in peace,
honoring her name from
sunrise to sunset,
they avowed never to forget
Terentia, a Queen so, so noble,
so loving, so brave,
that her body became mountain
and chose to save them all.

For generations upon generations,
millenia upon millenia,
all born called upon Terentia
every day
in gratitude.

CANTOS XVI:
Until, one day, it stopped.
Just like years that pass,
slow at first but then oh so fast,

the world began to forget
her sacrifice.

There soon came a time that Terentia
was but a faint memory
of an era that the world transcended,
vain in its pride,
equating, foolishly, antiquation to
advancement.

What was once forest-filled ranges,
Terentia's body now holds modernity
atop it:
paved roads, skyscrapers,
commerce and businesses.

CANTOS XVII:
I suppose it's to be understood,
then,
that the neighbors who make their homes
on her now,
look at her differently than the villagers once did,
so very long ago.

Incomprehensible, though, is how
new neighbors,
with all their knowings and technology,
and historical dating,
could view her feminine form,
supine,
with supple hips,
softened stomach,

swelling breasts,
remnants of long, long hair,
and ascertain her moniker to be:
Kings Mountain.

Terentia, she was no King,
she was greater than.
Her femininity swarmed around her
in everything that was good and true:
her strength, her softness,
her bravery, her altruism,
her compassion, her rage,
no, she was no King,
she was not a dictator demanding a throne,
not a tyrant bending those to her will,
not a talking head, taking,
no, not at all.

Her reign transcended all
in a manner that was pure,
true.
Her reign was a sacrifice,
perpetual, eternal,
in the name of love.

They call her King,
because they could not bear Queen.

Yet, it was her.
She was Woman.
She was Queen.
And, she still is.

CANTOS XVIII:
Terentia, Queen of the Mountain, may you rest in peace,
and we remember,
in your name:

Section V:

Should we just let it breathe

Schism

Like the sudden slicing of a limb—
when you left, I suddenly
appreciated your function.

I guess there was an amputation overnight.

Now, the mailbox sits full,
and the bed stays cold.
My heart hasn't beat since,
enwrapped in scar tissue
from your laceration.

It was probably two weeks,
of slicing and spiraling in
memories.
Memories that took me siege.

They fringed your cavity,
my helplessness.
They were splitting neural pathways,
with no anesthesia.
They were hopelessness,
wrapped up in despair.
They were endless.

Then, I made coffee.

My feet,
phantom limbs
wincing under weight,

were shored by floor.

I drifted to the kitchen, and
grazed my fingers
across the counter.
Strong, hard, wooden,
cool to the touch.

Running my nails across
the indentations,
I fantasized taking a knife to it.
Feeling the blade incise
the top of the surface:
a kind of visual representation of the
schism
that became us,
a world where I would not be
the only broken piece
in this home.

Then, the Keruig beeped,
and my thoughts diverged—
I need to check the mail.

Anxiously attached

It's not healthy to want to sew our skin together.
And yet,
I was happiest when you said that wasn't close enough—
you wanted to live in mine.

My bed
was where these conversations always happened.
I felt comfortable in my bed,
with you.
Like a cradle which held me,
I hoped you would hold me, too.

My bed offers a softness I need,
all the time,
always.
A reprieve, a retreat, a reset.
So, it makes sense the place
I felt the most natural
was where we would have these conversations.

I remember
the night of the Big Snow.

In my bed.
Fucking,
laughing, kissing, intermittently
in between moments
of Big Conversation.
We paused to leave the bed,
to step into the biting cold—

it didn't feel biting at all,
but soft and energizing, as the snow fell down.

You laid me down after
and spooned me
as I cried for the ache happiness brings alongside it;
I was so, so happy.
And yet,
I still braced for when our skin
would no longer be sewed together.

You didn't know why I was crying.

I scared you— the witnessing of my emotion.
The tears, the shakes, the sobs,
engulfing what I had to say,
the fear of the unsewing,
the fear of the break.

I was scared
but my fear roots me,
unlike you— whose fear causes you to flee.

It was our unsewing.

I was rooted in my cradle and you
fled,
ripping the sutures that bound us,
but somehow managing to ensure
I was the only one who felt the pain.

Seen

this is how you make someone feel seen:
pay attention, nod along;
ask leading questions;
hold their problems in your hands, stomach, throat;
remind them of what they forgot to do;
make sure you laugh because you're not a know-it-all;
ask for help, but only on things you know the answer to;
the help is for them, not for you;
show up;
sit down;
big spoon, calm in a storm;
driving the car;
this space, your space, is actually their space;
as a guest their needs are highest demand;
stroke their hair, their hand;
know when they're getting tired of being held;
never hold on longer than they want;

But okay, is this the time when I am able to be held?
when in your life have you ever needed to be held
It was when . . .
don't tell them because they don't need to know.

Should we just let it breathe

What were you really asking?
When you wanted to know:
if we should just let it breathe,
if it was too hard to be together?

I spun there, stuck,
trying to distinguish:
is our love
really hard, or
is our love
too hard?

Trapped somewhere in the grit between
really and *too,*
I racked my brain with reckoning:
I think I'm supposed to determine the difference.

(Should we just let it breathe?)

What does that look like?
The open air, inhalation,
the release from claustrophobia,
gasping lungs filling up,
after years of burning?
Exhaling the tension of always waiting
for the other shoe to drop?

But, listen, little lady, I know how to do hard.

I do hard every day.

I'd stand here with you,
for the rest of my life,
I'd stand here in hard,
welcoming battles and fine-tuning war songs,
but how do I know when
it's too hard?

Where's the line?
I haven't found it yet.
The boundary between
what I can do,
what's worth doing,
and what I should not have to?

(Should we just let it breathe?)

Hard is launch-party break-ups,
when you RSVP'd plus-one,
but left me solo, reciting at the mic
a love story, ours.

Hard is hearing you say
I still love you,
the second I was about to find love anew,
but, goddammit, knowing
I never stopped loving you, too.

(Should we just let it breathe?)

But those hards dilute down
when we talk about easy:
talk about cat cafes,

and crossword gifts,
and meeting in a kiss,
tangled up in cars, sofas, beds,
easy in the way your Moon fits mine,
and we mimic one another,
even when separated in space,
every fuckin' time.

(Should we just let it breathe?)

Your words were wasted—
I was stuck in the question which followed:
is it too hard?
You asked and I was trapped,
choking on carbon dioxide burning
from the wars we've fought before.

But, should we just let it breathe
is where my focus
should have been.

Box breaths reciting,
in *one-two-three-four*
hold one-two-three-four
out one-two-three-four
hold one-two-three-four,
neverending replay in the
hard that we are.

(Should we just let it breathe?)

(I don't think I can breathe without you, though.)

Tattoos

You are the only thing I live for.
Yet, I've never thought about dying more—

Even Galileo was condemned
for spinning us around
something greater.

I'm an empty container;
you're the shiny thing.

You touch my heart;
yet, I can't control
what it means.

I text you: let's get tatted
You say: i will but no animal ones
My response: moons

I love you,
I love you,
I love you.

I think I'll die instead.

Enough

So many of my cards on the table, the table's covered.
Decks obliterated, this goes beyond a hand.
Everything, even
down
to
my
soul,
is shown.

For so long, I've oscillated between
she loves me,
she loves me not—
between those paradigms,
of course it's the former.

Until now, I've focused on the ante
rather than cashing in on the bounty:
she doesn't love me enough.

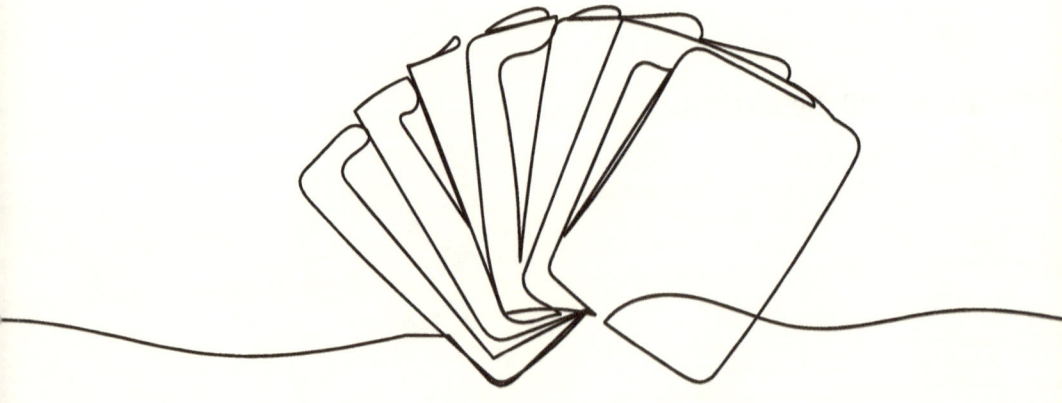

If love comes . . .

"If love comes, it's going to have to knock me on my ass."

Onlookers will chuckle when I make statements like these.
"She's fierce.
Independent.
Knows what she wants and won't accept less."

I love to think that's how they perceive me.

What they don't know:
on my 27th birthday, I spoke with a
psychic.
I didn't care
when,
where,
how,
who,
my love was.

The question I asked?
*"Will I know that they're the person with whom
I'm meant to be?"*

No, I need to be knocked on my ass
because
the insanity rutting down my heart
fears . . .

*that I won't see my person if they're standing
right in front of me.*

Section VI:

Call it what you want to

Gremlin

I pulled a gremlin
out of my throat
and she was purple.

Slick and matted,
bits of hair clung to her,
rogue and sporadic.

She had a small,
childlike voice,
thin and squeaky.

She wasn't cleaned.
Dirty.
Due to neglect.

She said she needed
love.
And acceptance.

The gremlin cried easily
when she didn't get attention.
She wasn't callous
from the care she hadn't received
it just made her
want care
more and more.

Greedy,
ravenous for love.

Greedy,
for attention and devotion.

Disgust singed at
my face
when I first saw her.
It pulled the edges of my mouth
taut,
nostrils flared.

That feeling pulled wrong
at my body,
alien, foreign.

Then, divinely, my body softened.
Holy and true, my jaw loosened.
Compassion made itself known.
Relieving revulsion, and
purifying instead.

I pulled a gremlin
out of my throat,
held her in my hand,
and stayed with her.

We sat skin-to-skin.
We rocked and learned
each other well,
like new friends do.

I let her cry until
I worried she'd wash away.

But she never did.

Persistent, my gremlin
rooted herself down—
a novice to warmth,
she swaddled my fondness
around her.

Do you see her now?

She's cleaned and
cared for,
purple body cleansed.

Her hair is full,
bright and polished.

She's still voracious
for love, attention, devotion—
That is unchanging.
And, that is okay.

I won't leave her.

Non dividemur, nisi a morte.
We shall not be separated, except by death.

The weight of walls

Brick by brick,
I built a wall
around my heart.
Years of safety,
but oh-so heavy.

Now, *I begin to break it down.*

Kin

My house was built in the late 1800s—
parts of it, anyway.
Generations of Southern Baptists,
men that were called preachers,
good men,
powerful men,
women that were called whores,
difficult women,
crazy women,
made their home in this house.

I am of these men and women.

Women that nursed babies,
and rocked the *very big emotions*
that raged their little bodies,
men that saw the sin of the world,
and felt it in their bones,
as they tried really, really hard
to shield themselves,
their women, and
their little babies' bodies from it.

I am of these men and women.
So, indeed, is this home— parts of it, anyway.

This home has seen
shame and persecution
and these walls have held
secret desires and wants and needs

that were oh-so-too-big for the world they were in.

A century ago, the men and women
in this home pushed
their dreams
down, down, down,
into the fibers of their DNA and
shunned what they wanted
for that which they *should do.*

A century later, I have made this home different.

Where once there were the Commandments of
a Lord painted to be
hellfire, brimstone, perdition, and punishment,
there are now psalms that hold
incantations of the Feminine Divine.
A softness-in-Her-strength, accepting-those-who-yearn-to-grow,
Goddess,
Whose Image
I Am Modeled After.

Where once there were
rods and hickory sticks,
branches used as tools to teach
punishment, retribution, obedience,
there are now pages and pages of words,
daring the holder to break the bonds that have held back
growth, home, self, awareness, alignment.

How do you want to show up in the world?
How can your hands mold your reality into that for which

you want to be, see, know, and love?

The men and women in this home once
worked,
and pushed,
and planned,
and fit,
so that I could
expand-simmer-dream-hope-*be.*

But, I can't break the generational trauma
without first
thanking that which
got
me
here:

Thank you to those men and women.
May your bones rest in peace
and spirit and soul dance
around desires reclaimed.

My body was made to move

Did you know your body can fly?

Phalanges can grip
elements
in the air,
under the ground,
through the sea,

to transport you through and to

$$\textit{Time and Space.}$$

We weren't made, my love, to be stagnant
creatures
holding down a fort,
never leaving the room.

Give me a ground I can run on so fast
that I swear I'll join the birds above me.
I'll tunnel down soil so rich as
I hold myself, happy baby,
stretch and turn, I'll transcend:
My body was made to move.

Water in the wilderness

Oh, old soul, I'm ancient.
I've a heart like water.
Filling the gaps, nestling in crevices,
running through and into
anywhere that is desperate for
hydration.

Dry, deep split lips are my speciality.

Sometimes I feel I was made to take up space
in environments that are
one step away from obliteration.

The places others are afraid to go:
one step away from
purely fucking (un-in-habit-able).

Uh, but . . . in my habit, I am able.

Give me a desert, and I'll raise you a rainforest.

They are rooted

I couldn't tell you how many trees surround my home.
They're everywhere.
Standing regal and consistent beside one another,
tall, sturdy blades of big grass—
they hold their ground.

They are rooted, and they flow.

Their rigidity I can relate to, occupying space
in a way which will not budge.

Ever present, ever unchanging.

Their fluidity I grapple with, allowing the breeze to
squeeze between
each leaf,
wiggling and moving with the wind.

Malleable and discerning,
why trap in amber branches that desire to play?

I am rooted, and I [ache to] flow.

My fiercest protector

Today, I'm going to be happy.
Today, I'm going to be well.
Today, I'm going to trust myself.

AT LEAST 4 KILLED IN GEORGIA HIGH SCHOOL SHOOTING

You trust you, you love you, you're kind to you.

Isn't it a funny thing to have to fill
myself up with these platitudes?
To have a chance of making it through the day?

*HURRICANE HELENE'S DAMAGE, RELATED EXPENSES
IN NORTH CAROLINA SHATTERING RECORDS,
ESTIMATED AT $53 BILLION*

I don't think we were meant to live this way.

When I asked myself what to do with myself,
a voice inside whispered,
you are your fiercest protector.

"What am I to protect?"
I scream back.

*TRUMP'S "BORDER CZAR" DETAILS PLANS TO REINTRODUCE
MIGRANT FAMILY DETENTION CENTERS*

How am I supposed to go about life
when I'm cursed with the knowing that nothing is right?

The bodies and the bombs and the economy and
the fucking election.

My skin crawls when I try to be.

*SYRIANS SEARCH FOR LOVED ONES WHO VANISHED
UNDER ASSAD REGIME*

I try to turn myself inwards.

You trust you, you love you, you're kind to you.

Gripping hard onto these words like deliverances, freeing me.

WHAT COULD 3 DEGREES C OF WARMING LOOK LIKE?

A fierce protector can be a voice which booms,
a roar as you rise.
A soft turn, or
a gentle start.
A simple sentence.

"What am I to protect?"
I ask again, slowly.

A reply:
Your trust, your love, your kindness.

In a pregnant moment, clarity buds and Today blooms.

In comfort, in growth

There are places I am comfortable.

Give me a piece of paper,
and a pen,
an empty room, and low low light:
I will create all the beautiful, mesmerizing images you need.
Words dripping
off my fingers, like honey.

Give me a problem to be solved,
daring as if a challenge
that lives in an open arena, waiting to be met.
I will meet it—
answers erupting
through me, like a goldrush.

There are places I am uncomfortable, too.

Drop me in a nursery,
imp in a crib,
arms flailing and legs jetset on taking off:
I'll drop to the floor.
Mimicking movements, *what should I do here?*

Drop me in front of a camera,
Janus on a tripod,
reflective that of which I truly am:
I'll flee from the scene.
Rushing run, *how do I appear here?*

we're creatures of habit—
creatures of comfort,
routine and process,
boxes and organization.

I box my understanding of myself away,
label: DEFINED.

Definitions evolve, though.
Boxes burst, and
organization unorders.

In my comfort I am larger-than-life,
grand and stunning,
impressive and insurmountable.
In my discomfort I am growing shyly,
swaying step-by-shaken-step.
In comfort, there is certitude.
In discomfort, there is profundity.

We are not fragile

We are not fragile ornaments,
not glass that shatters.
We are strong, resilient,
crafted to bend,
to hold love,
and give it freely—
without fear.

Lives in a pause

I can write sad.

I can write sad, really, really well.
But, I don't need sad right now.

I need hope.

I need an underneath,
background
beat
that breaks internal monologue.

Something that swells forth.

Slow down, you crazy child.
Without hearing it,
I catch myself—
thinking the song
the entire time.

For just one second,
I need to be able to separate myself
from my heartbreak,
from my pain,
from my sadness,
the worthlessness of it all . . .
to something else, something bigger.

What lives within the pause?

The whole damn occasion

Oh fierce soul, how can I help you understand
the power of your stillness?

Moving, moving,
acting,
pushing.

I commend you on your motions, but, darling, they are finite.

Do you really think all you bring to the table
is the cloth laid atop it?
You are not just the dish that held the meat,
or solely the spoon that introduced the spice to the starch.

No, powerful soul, you are
the whole damn occasion.

The creator, the digester, and the sustenance.

How does it feel to be every variable,
every role,
housed inside
the same flesh?

Receive This Sacred Truth:
Choose Your Collective.

Queen of air and knowing

Finger the card's bounds.
Let the edge's sturdiness
imprint into your ridges.
Altering your DNA,
so your encoding
explodes forth—heightened.

The cards themselves are worn well,
used countless times,
by countless fools,
bartering coins for platitudes.
At least that's what some, granted, most, are there for.

You, though.
You aren't.

Feast your eyes on those strong lines
that carve Her stature:
An arched eyebrow,
shoulders pulled back, neck high, and blades touching—
her body mimics the sword she carries.

The Queen of Air.

She you and you Her,
the butterfly wings sprouting out Her back
juxtapose:
for all her strength, many wonder aloud,
there's no way this woman can soar.
She peers back, head cocked, asking:

Do you dare ask questions,
begging for answers,
of what you cannot conceive?
Shall I really show you what my power achieves?

They were mistaken.

Her mind scales heights angels cannot reckon,
cutting through space and time,
polished and seasoned,
Her I'd always bet on
against any mortal soul's reason.

Find Her in any tarot deck,
signaling with intellect
only found in cosmos,
words of which
even interpreter
cannot comprehend.

Allow Her to flap wings off the face,
extracting spirit from page that She, for a moment,
allowed to contain.
Feel Her pass the fingerprints that held Her,
and into you, engrained.

Find Her now, leaving the room.
She you and you Her,
winged-creatures of divinity:
as your birthright, now you soar.

You always knew how.

Beautifully self-involved

When I'm my favorite part of me,
the best, the most, the happiest I can be,
the air glitters in the morning-time.

My cats are fed as they blink the
sleep from their eyes,
the same time I do.
Puttering around my feet, they meow and purr,
requesting to feel the hot mug
I hold in my hands,
black coffee and milk.

At the foot of my bed, I criss-cross,
applesauce my legs
and put pen to paper.
Beautifully self-involved, those morning musings
are always about me.
What to do today?
What is work going to entail?
Dare I write a quick prayer for an easy day?
Purging all my worries and concerns,
I allow them to fill a space where they can stay.

Then, I focus on the good stuff.

My morning-time thoughts follow some type of theme:
anxiety over relationships,
fear of what is to come,
desire to try something new.

I'm pretty gifted at fixation:
My mind can compartmentalize
itself in a ghastly way.
This morning's obsession:
my stressed state.

I choose the morning theme; I heal myself from it.

The air around me glitters in the morning-time.

A final sip of coffee,
and a "closed eye moment"
lights me up inside.
Tension can still arise,
and the familiar rush of
what's-the-time bargaining
can rear its ugly head.

And, yet, I know this investment pays off.

If I tell you I meditate every morning,
please understand I am no expert here.
I am no pro at silencing the thoughts in my head,
but I am brilliant at discerning those that should pass by
and those that hold further inspection.

To the untrained eye, I'm not doing it "right."
More often than not, there's no stillness.
Frequently I am rocking back and forth,
feeling the heels of my feet,
even audibly groaning—
releasing something deep down inside me.

And, ironically, getting it out *fills me up*.

While I am no pro at the art of meditation,
I am brilliant when it comes to my mornings.
Every time.

When I wake up hating my anxiety,
I meditate with hands cupping my face.
Celebrating every time I can make my belly bigger,
and fill up more and more with an inhale.
Feeling the eventual upturn of my cheeks against my palms,
and a slow, small smile
that brims at my lips,
I exhale the concern that tore at me for so many decades of my life.

Every morning is a new revelation—
or appreciation.
On the truly special mornings,
my entire body will tingle.
Starting at the base of the spine,
a vibration moves its entire way up
and *holy hell, world, watch out.*

Those are the days I'm fairly certain I will change the world,
challenging the open air in front of me:
"Hey, world, wanna see what I can do?"

The air around me glitters in the morning-time.

I am in no way living the perfect life,
nor claiming to be a perfect individual.
I am very, very flawed, one hundred percent of the time.

And every day I pray
to *perfect*
just one more breath
than I did the day before.

Honoring the morning's beauty ensures, most of the time, I do.

There are times the day still feels draining.
Combining my introverted-empathic demeanor
with a job that requires me to
convince people of something half the day,
and fix their problems the other half,
takes a large toll.

But, the game-changer is this:
I am starting the day at one hundred percent.
Before I speak to any one person,
before I fix one problem,
before I convince someone to do any one thing,
I show up for myself.

I wrap myself in love,
and affirmation,
and observation.

Then, I go do the damn thing.

Before, I was starting the day
on an empty tank
and begging myself to fly on fumes.

Now, the air around me glitters in the morning-time.

The armor we wear

A guarded heart,
sharp tongue slices.
Years of metal,
heavy on my neck.
Now, I *unlearn*.

Not for beauty

I planned the day
without a thought,
a photoshoot
to catch the light,
scribbled to-do lists,
a safety net,
still dread crept in
overnight.

Would the camera
see me clear,
or would my flaws
begin to show?
Pale skin,
the weight,
angles off;
fears that refused to let go.

But then a phrase began to hum,
rolling gently through my head:
I am beautiful as I am,
because I look like me.

I closed my eyes,
breathed in deep,
and let the dread fall like a sigh.
With purpose, I posed
in the morning sun:
not for beauty, but to try.

Rose-colored glasses

My cats stomp paws in the morning.
Mewl for mealtime breakfast,
even though they're far from the
hunger they express.

They never reason that this
cry-wolf will make me love them less,
never logic that I might not want them
to take up space
on my chest,
or that maybe, just maybe,
my yarn is my yarn
and not one of their toys
to mischievously mangle during
evening simple-joys.

My cats exist in a rose-colored world.
Where they've only ever known—
full certainty—
they are loved and cared for,
fervently.

A world that comprises
of delights
in little paws stomping,
soft bodies plopping,
with urgent meows,
that the time for 4 AM breakfast
is actually *right now*.

Today I might borrow
their rose-colored glasses,
and live in a world
that I, just for today,
believe
loves me back.

Hot yoga, cool thoughts

I keep my house at sixty-eight degrees, year round—
cold is my comfort.

But there I was,
in a room over one hundred,
humidity heavy,
my first yoga class.

Eyes wide, breath shallow,
I caught my reflection,
something I spent years avoiding.

You don't belong here.

My body was too large, too red,
sweat pouring,
hair frizzing out of place.
The instructor's voice called:
"Keep eye contact with yourself."

But my mind was louder:
you are too big, too clumsy.

You don't fit in here.

I closed my eyes.
What would it be like to let it all go?
I released,
just for a moment.

When eyes opened again,
I heard something new,
a voice quiet, yet steady.

You can release it here.

Cobra pose, my palms slick yet glued
to a borrowed mat.
Obsidian t-shirt camouflaging
puddles of sweat,
pooling and hydrating—
my sternum met the mirrored wall.

Be where you're at here.

I left the class,
body buzzing,
and watched snow fall:
a quiet release,
a letting go
I hadn't known I needed.

Wildflowers of love

Resilient souls,
strong, unbreakable:
we give a fuck.
Toss love like wildflowers,
even in the face of fear.

Call it what you want to

Da-dum. Da-dum. Da-duh, da-duh.
Dum.
Dum.
Dum.

I marvel most days to be both
in and of the Universe.

Looking at you, I see eons
splayed across your face.
Every pore of your skin is
both supernova and earthquake.
Combusting, releasing,
producing, devastating,
in and of the Universe.

You are made of stuff much stronger
than consciousness can comprehend—
in and of the Universe.

Your eyes beg of me to answer that which stays
on the tip of your seafoam-pressed tongue:
"What in the world do I do next?"

In the Universe, you sit on bones that are built
upon both calamity and miracle.
Of the Universe, you are both disaster and disaster's Divine.

What in the world do you do next?

My dear.
Whatever the fuck you want.

Acknowledgments

This poetry collection would never have happened if I didn't step foot into Dr. Shana Hartman's Intro to English course in 2011. You've been my professor, my boss, my life coach, and now my book coach. Happiest I am to say, you're my friend. Thank you for all you've done for me; it is universes more than you'll ever know.

Thank you, Dr. Cindy Urbanski, you reach the maximum for what pure love looks like in human form. Thank you for reading my words and making sense of them when I forgot what I was trying to say.

Thank you, Melisa Graham: you are utter brilliancy. A Design Goddess. And someone who just speaks pure truth, every time.

Thank you, Mom and Dad, for never, ever letting me believe I couldn't do something.

Thank you, Aubry Edwards, for showing me what it means to be a good person.

Thank you, Gracey Edwards, for showing me what it means to be a good adult.

Thank you, Mallory Edwards, for showing me what it means to be a good writer.

Thank you Bingley & Darcy, your cat cuddles ensured I've always made it out alive. Mawmaw Sharon, for writing my stories down when I was too young to do anything but spew them aloud. Pawpaw Larry, for planting tulips and choosing me. Carrissa Brown, for giving me Adeline and the absolute safest space I've ever known: forever beside you. Dylan Rudisill, for still playing cards with me on cold floors, even decades later. Jana Tindall, for giving me the best secret I've ever been tasked with keeping. Andrew Woods, for virtual sanctuaries every four to six weeks, where I can be even the hardest parts of myself. Taylor Swift, for helping the world remember that poetry *never* went out of style.

And, thank you to everyone else who has tried to teach me something— I promise I listened.

About the Author

Taylor Edwards is a poet, writer, and eternal seeker of connection through words. With a Master of Arts in Integrated Marketing Communications and a background in English Education, Taylor blends creativity with a passion for structure, bringing clarity and depth to her writing. Her work reflects a lifelong journey of learning, teaching, and embodying the transformative power of language.

When she's not crafting verses or managing creative projects, Taylor can be found spoiling her two purr-fect cats or diving into stories that inspire new ideas. Her poetry explores the interplay of identity, resilience, and the human experience, offering readers a space to feel seen and heard.

Connect with Taylor and discover more of her work by following her on socials: @tayloredwardspoetry.